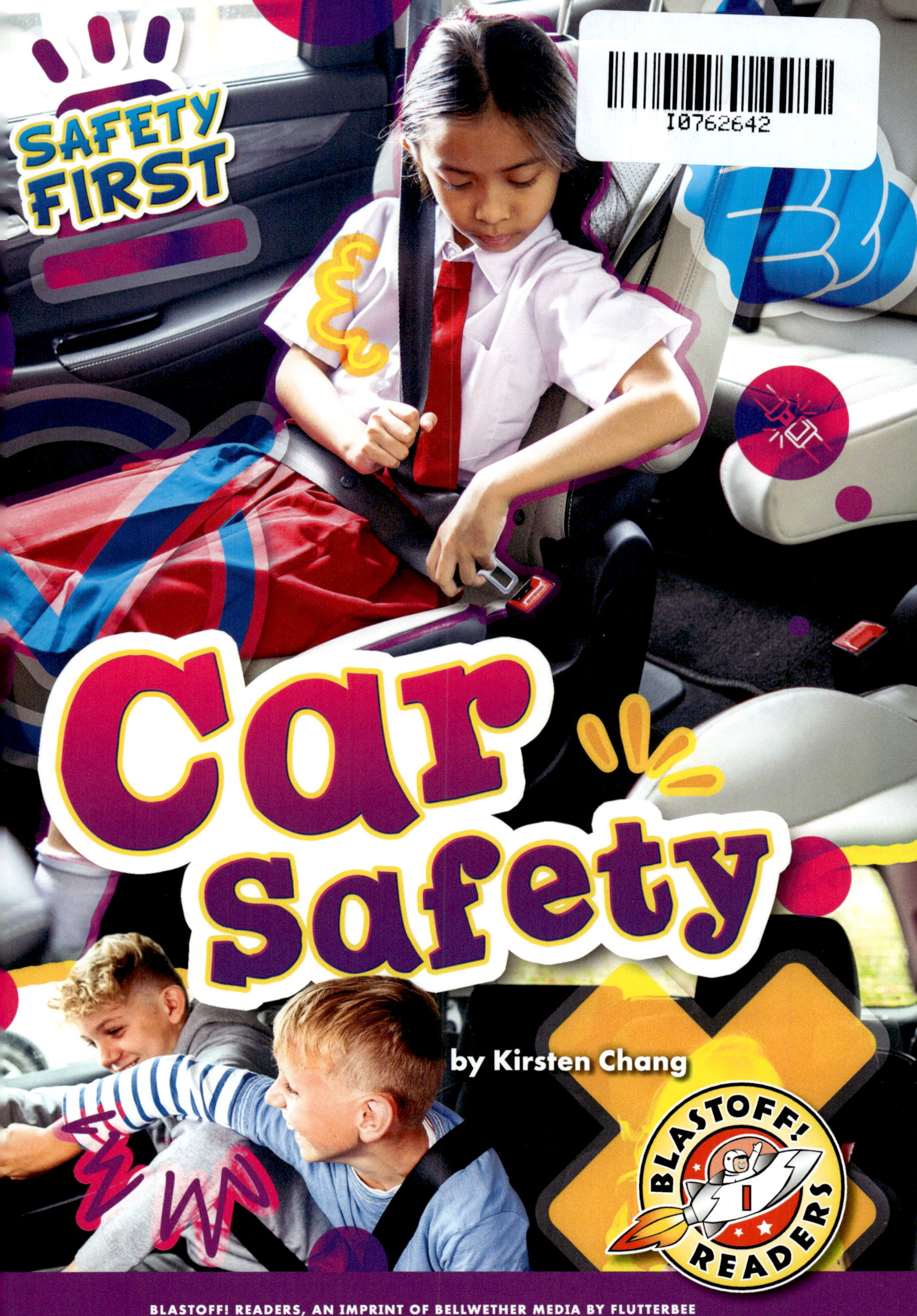

BLASTOFF! READERS, AN IMPRINT OF BELLWETHER MEDIA BY FLUTTERBEE

Blastoff! Readers are carefully developed by literacy experts to build reading stamina and move students toward fluency by combining standards-based content with developmentally appropriate text.

Level 1 provides the most support through repetition of high-frequency words, light text, predictable sentence patterns, and strong visual support.

Level 2 offers early readers a bit more challenge through varied sentences, increased text load, and text-supportive special features.

Level 3 advances early-fluent readers toward fluency through increased text load, less reliance on photos, advancing concepts, longer sentences, and more complex special features.

★ **Blastoff! Universe**

Reading Level

Grade K

Grades 1–3

Grade 4

This edition first published in 2027 by Bellwether Media, Inc.

For information regarding permission, write to Bellwether Media, Inc., Attention: Permissions Department, 3500 American Blvd W, Suite 150, Bloomington, MN 55431.

Library of Congress Cataloging-in-Publication Data is available at www.loc.gov or upon request from the publisher.

ISBN: 9798898800369 (hardcover)
ISBN: 9798898802899 (paperback)
ISBN: 9798898801601 (ebook)

Editor: Rachael Barnes Designer: Andrea Schneider

Printed in the United States of America, North Mankato, MN.

Table of Contents

Road Safety

Maria sits on her booster seat. Her seat belt is **buckled**. Road trips are fun!

booster seat
seat belt

Why Stay Safe?

Cars take us many places. **Accidents** can happen on the road.

accident

Heavy **traffic** can be **dangerous**. We could get **injured** in a crash.

injured arm
traffic
24 HOUR PARKING

We follow rules.
We stay safe.
We keep others safe!

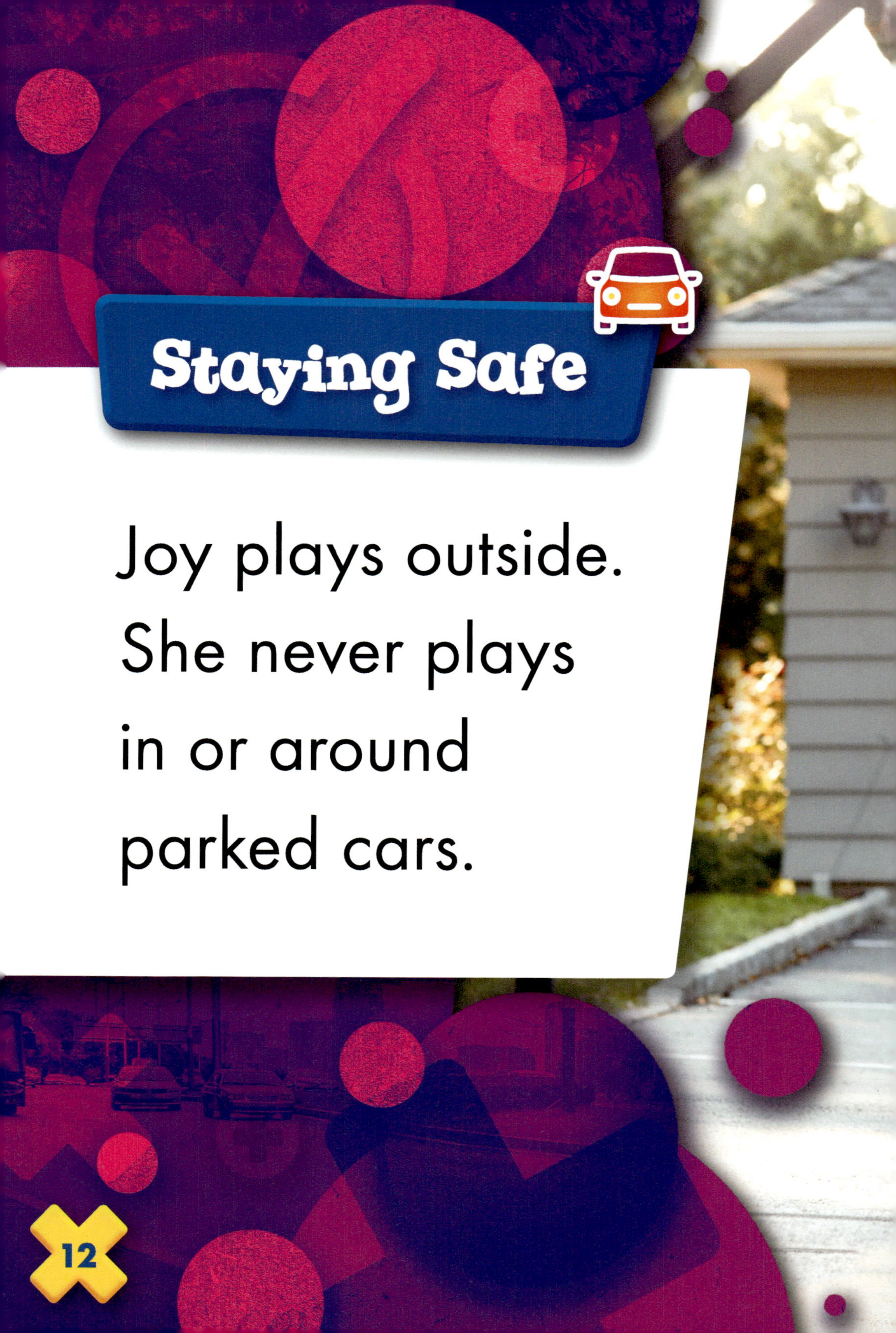

Staying Safe

Joy plays outside. She never plays in or around parked cars.

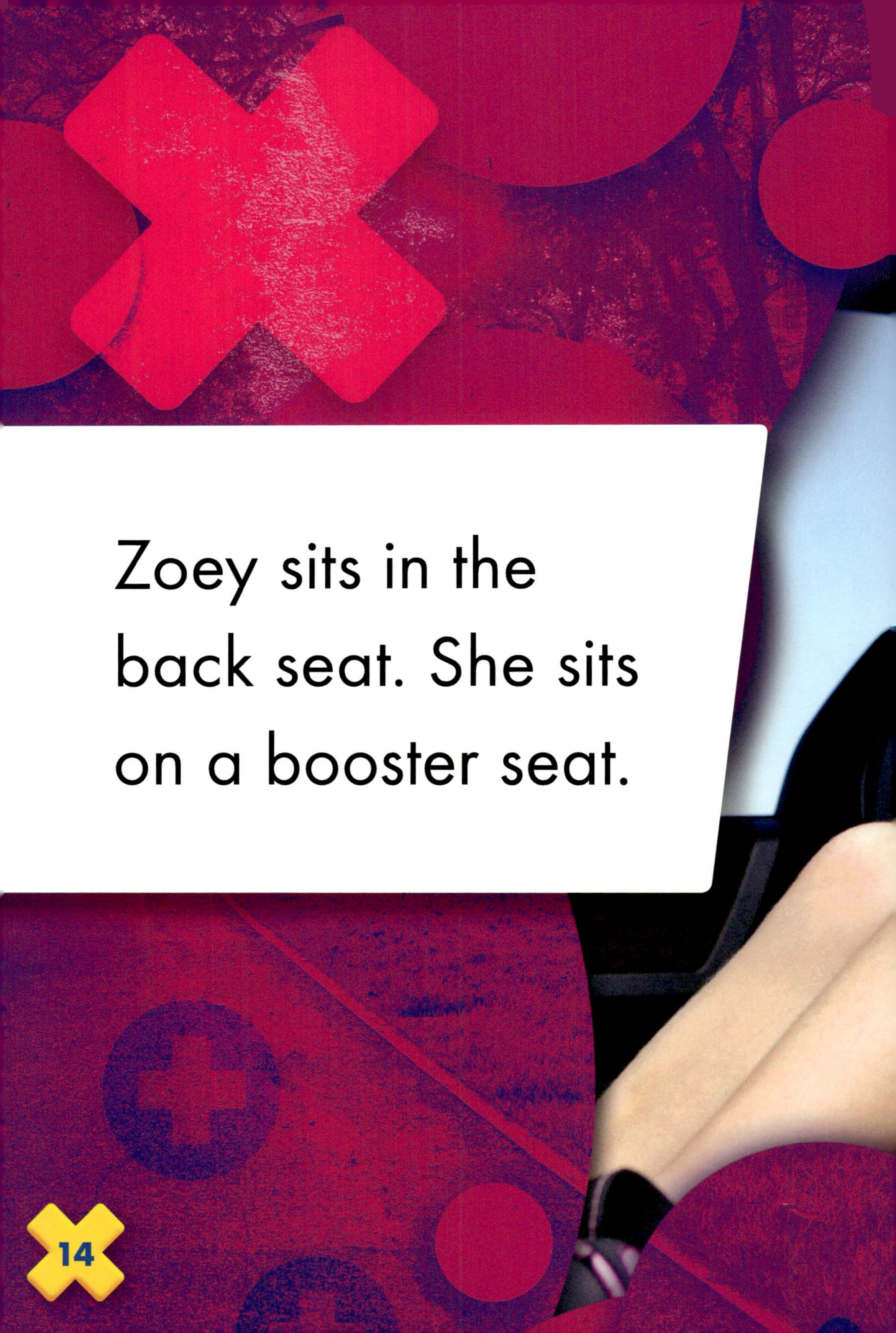

Zoey sits in the back seat. She sits on a booster seat.

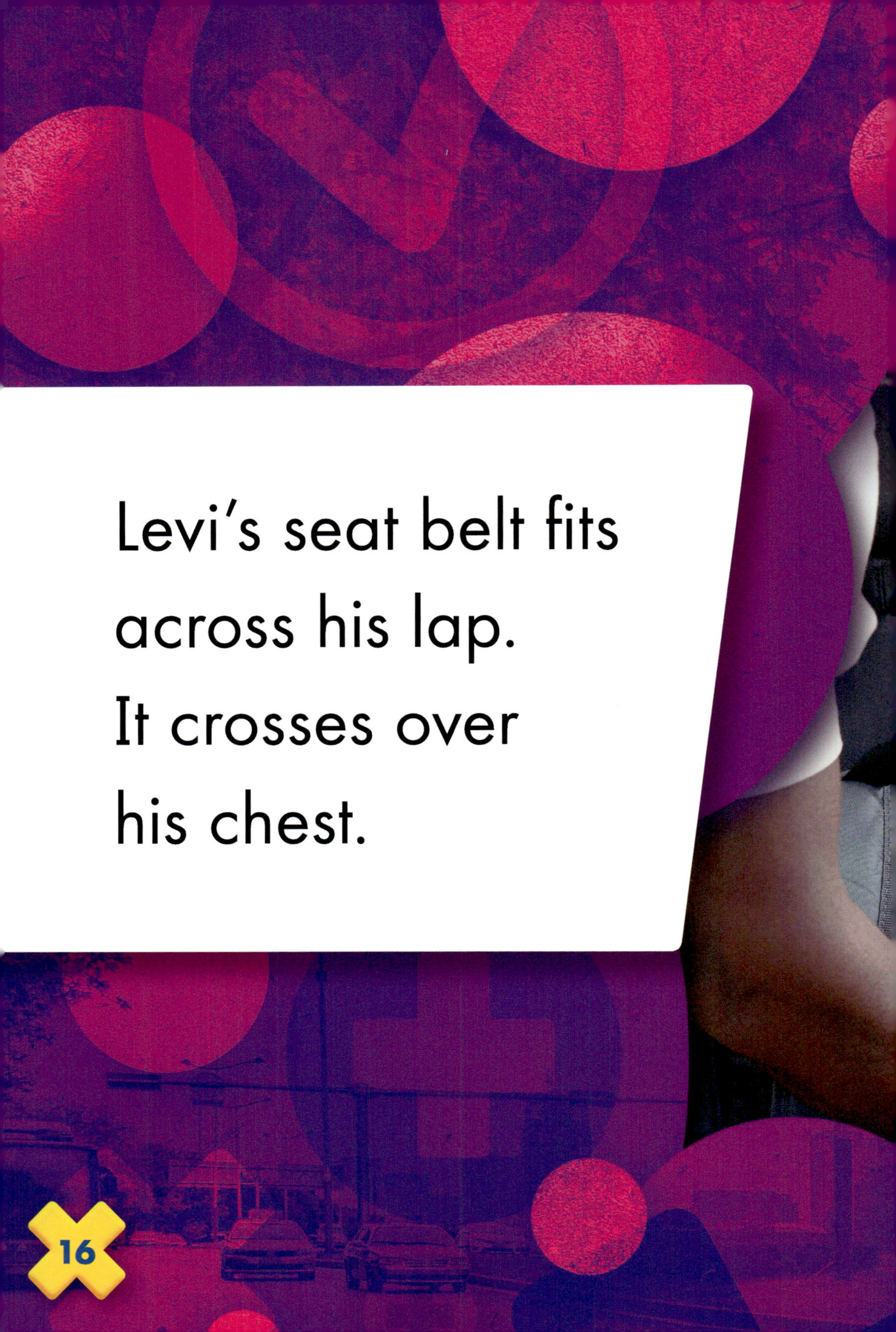

Levi's seat belt fits across his lap. It crosses over his chest.

How to Use a Seat Belt

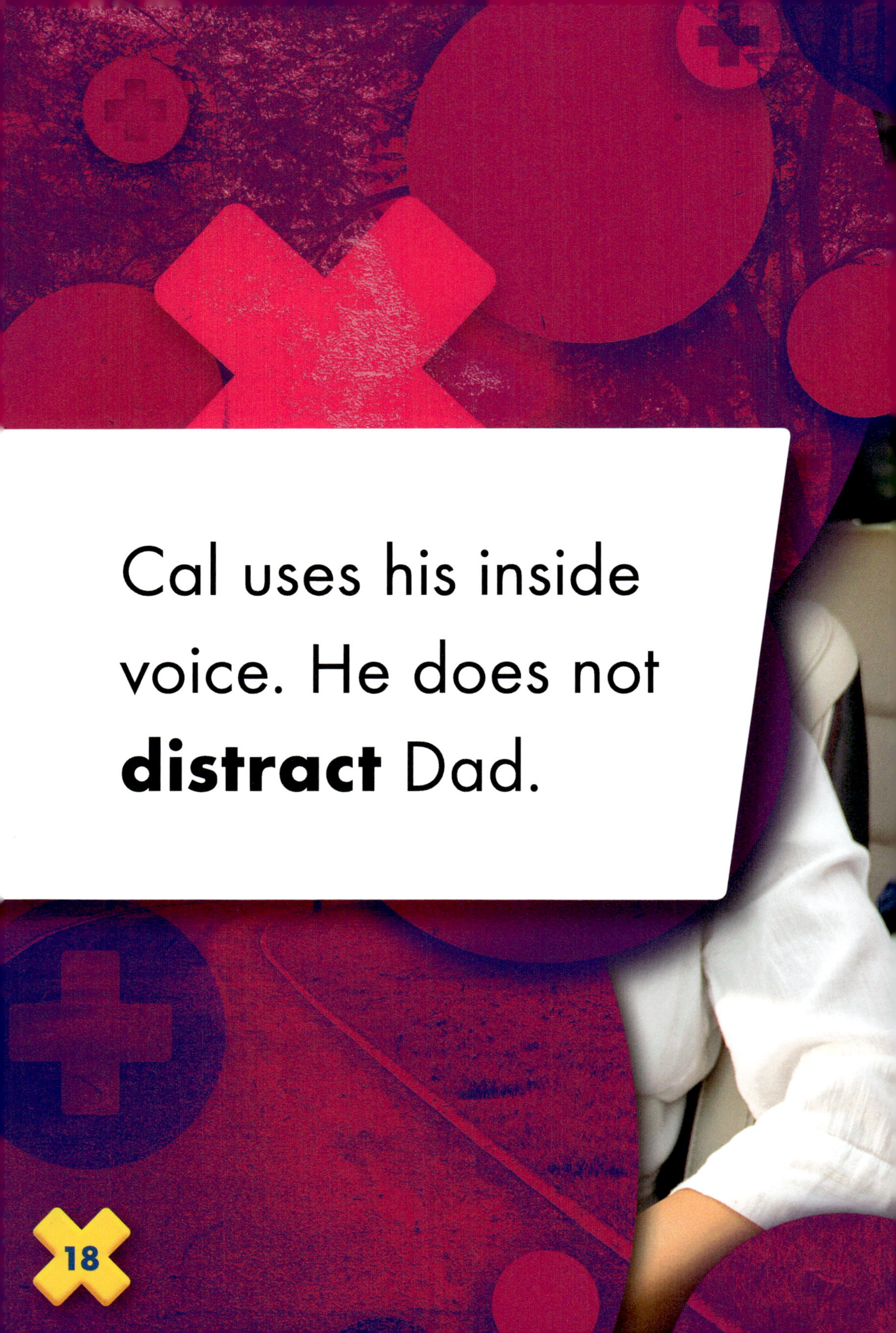

Cal uses his inside voice. He does not **distract** Dad.

Ann waits for Mom to open the car door. They made it home safely!

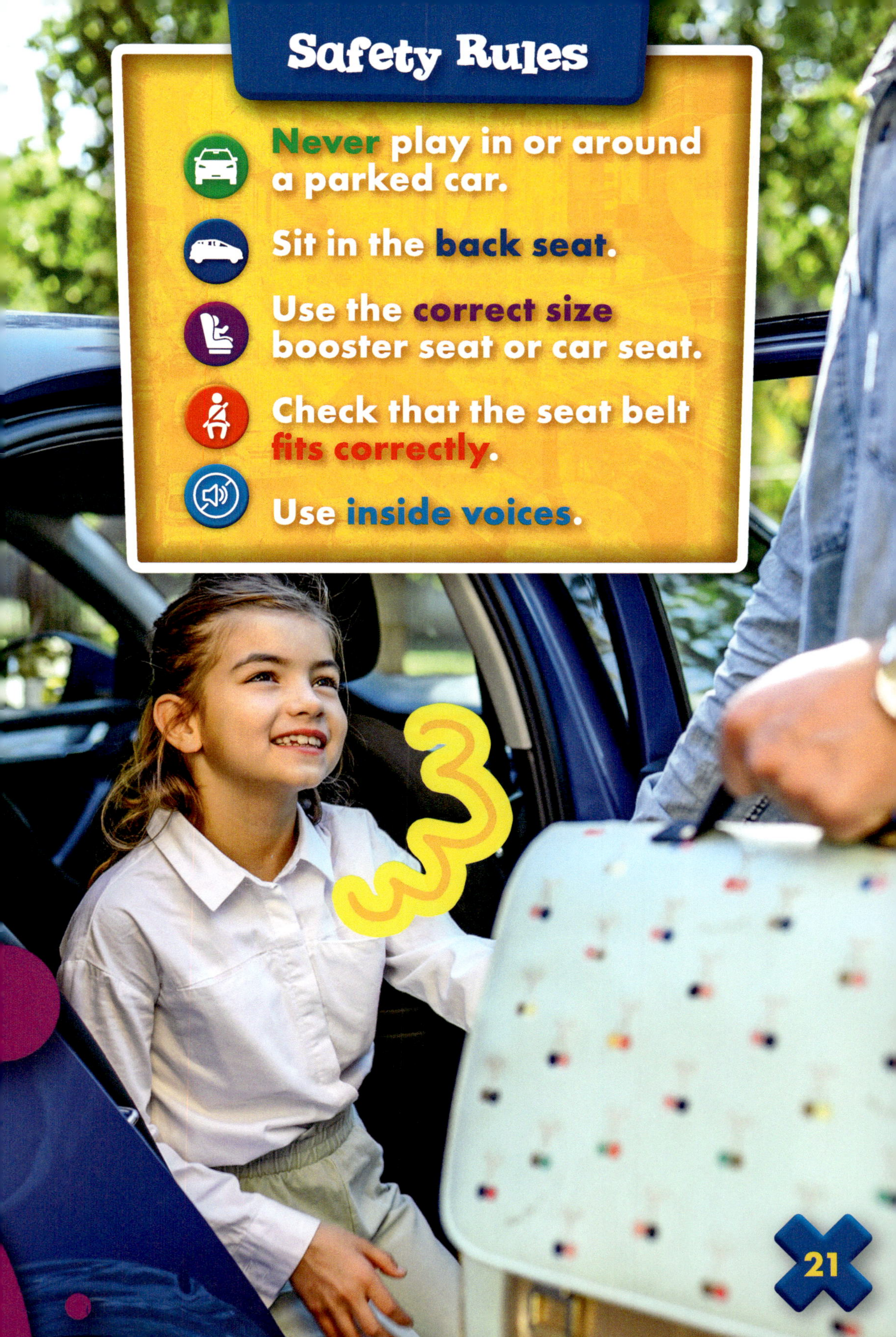
Safety Rules
Never play in or around a parked car.
Sit in the back seat.
Use the correct size booster seat or car seat.
Check that the seat belt fits correctly.
Use inside voices.

Glossary

accidents

sudden events in which someone is hurt

buckled

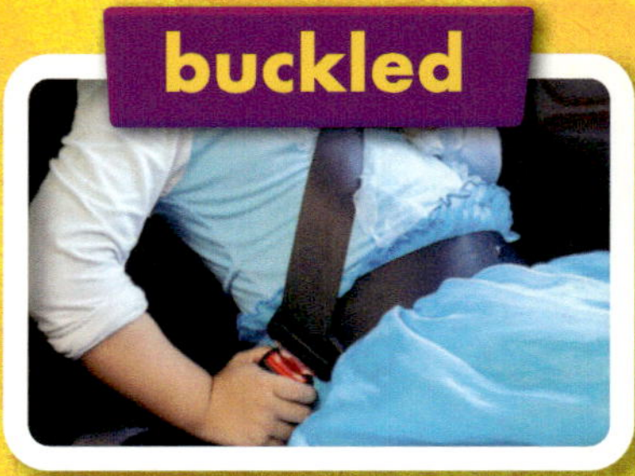

held together

dangerous

not safe

distract

to take someone's attention away from something

injured

hurt

traffic

the movement of people and vehicles along a street

To Learn More

AT THE LIBRARY

Catena, Melissa. *Road Safety.* Minneapolis, Minn.: Jump!, 2025.

Chang, Kirsten. *Street Safety.* Minneapolis, Minn.: Bellwether Media, 2027.

Emminizer, Theresa. *Staying Safe on the Road.* Buffalo, N.Y.: PowerKids Press, 2023.

ON THE WEB

FACTSURFER

Factsurfer.com gives you a safe, fun way to find more information.

1. Go to www.factsurfer.com.
2. Enter "car safety" into the search box and click 🔍.
3. Select your book cover to see a list of related content.

Index

The images in this book are reproduced through the courtesy of: Leo Lintang, front cover (top); SolStock, front cover (bottom); Chaaim, p. 3 (car seat); Kuzmick, p. 3 (car); Hispanolistic, pp. 4-5; bilanol, pp. 6-7; agsaz, pp. 8-9; Kzenon, pp. 9 (inset), 22 (injured); Sait Aydin, pp. 10-11; Monkey Business Images, pp. 12-13; Viktor Cvetkovic, p. 13 (inset); sirtravelalot, pp. 14-15; Himalayan Pics/ Alamy Stock Photo, pp. 16-17; Olena Miroshnichenko, pp. 18-19, 22 (distract); bluecinema, pp. 20-21; hodim, p. 22 (accidents); jittawit.21, p. 22 (buckled); standret, p. 22 (dangerous); Joel Villanueva, p. 22 (traffic); Destina, p. 23.